W. E. B. Du Bois: The Life and Legacy of Early 20th Century America's Most Famous Civil Rights Activist

By Charles River Editors

About Charles River Editors

Charles River Editors provides superior editing and original writing services across the digital publishing industry, with the expertise to create digital content for publishers across a vast range of subject matter. In addition to providing original digital content for third party publishers, we also republish civilization's greatest literary works, bringing them to new generations of readers via ebooks.

Sign up here to receive updates about free books as we publish them, and visit Our Kindle Author Page to browse today's free promotions and our most recently published Kindle titles.

Introduction

W. E. B. Du Bois

"Once we were told: Be worthy and fit and the ways are open. Today the avenues of advancement in the army, navy, and civil service, and even in business and professional life, are continually closed to black applicants of proven fitness, simply on the bald excuse of race and color." – Du Bois, 1908

The abiding question of slavery's legality in the United States loomed over its pursuit of independence from Great Britain. Rather than proceeding with a partial union, Congress required a unanimous vote on Thomas Jefferson's "Declaration," and so proceeded with a divided one. Unanimity on the document's merit was at that time otherwise unobtainable, as southern industry relied on the slave trade in Africa and the Caribbean, with the support of northern shipping. The issue was shelved in the hope that the union, once established, would resolve the matter amicably during a period of more amenable circumstances, and that the African-American would remain in an accepting state for the duration. Passages referring to the practice of slavery were struck from Jefferson's final draft. American founding fathers fully realized that the Declaration's assertion of equal citizenship would be viewed as hypocrisy until such a time that consensus could be reached, but nevertheless retained the fatal flaw within their concretization of the new union. Trusting in the evolution of social enlightenment to heal the fracture between northern and southern colonies soon after, many were disappointed to see that the Constitution enacted in the following decade fared no better than Jefferson's paper, further hardening the status of nonwhites in the new United States. Nearly a century after the first unified governmental resistance against the crown of England, the chasm of interior strife widened to the point of war. The condition of the American of African descent was in several aspects worse than at any time during the eighteenth century.

Despite a Union victory and Lincoln's Emancipation Proclamation, unthinkable in the previous century, a new form of suppression and violence descended on the African-American population. "Reconstruction" is employed as a generic term for the period that followed the American Civil War. Suggesting a successful rejuvenation of a war-ravaged South, it lamentably gave way to a resurrection of the same white ruling class and slave-owner mentality, protecting the status quo in the legislatures and courts. With the distortion of Reconstruction's intent came a body of racial policy and a tacitly understood social code that barred the pre-war slave class from personal freedom and opportunity, at the risk of great personal violence for anyone who objected. The arduous task of overthrowing Jim Crow codes and legislation marked one of the first strides toward the modern struggle for ethnic equality in American society and required nearly a century of struggle.

That effort spawned a multitude of heroic African-American activists, but it is remembered in large part for the work of two iconic African-American men of stature. Much like their later counterparts, Reverend Martin Luther King, Jr. and Malcolm X, the debate between gradual integration through temporary accommodation and overtly insistent activism was led by Booker T. Washington and W. E. B. Du Bois. Through the last years of the 19th century, Washington's gentler approach of enhancing black prospects through vocational education, largely accomplished with white permission and funds, seemed the popular choice. His legacy can be sensed in King's subsequent willingness to extend an olive branch to white Americans in a sense of unity, although Washington's propensity for accommodation held no place in King's ministry.

Ultimately, however, the vision that oversaw the creation of the Tuskegee Institute faded in the early 20th century as black intellectualism and stiffening resolve came to the fore. This side's greatest proponent, William Edward Burghardt Du Bois, still stands among the greatest and most controversial minds of any black leader in his country. The first African-American to receive a doctorate from Harvard University, Du Bois rose to become one of the most important social thinkers of his time in a 70-year career of combined scholarship, teaching, and activism. His lifelong efforts were devoted to the immediate acceptance of African-Americans as full citizens in good standing, and to the universal dismissal of white superiority. A co-founder of the National Association for the Advancement of Colored People, Du Bois was involved with virtually every equality-oriented organization of note in the early and mid-20th century, and his legacy can be found in a long line of extraordinary black scholars extending to the present day.

Although Du Bois' name is still (and somewhat inexplicably) less well-known than that of Washington, his prolific writings serve as a bedrock to the modern social engines at work in the pursuit of racial equality in America. In his life and experience of nearly a century, he spanned the administrations of Andrew Johnson and Lyndon Baines Johnson, dying only one day before King's "I Have a Dream" speech.

W. E. B. Du Bois: The Life and Legacy of Early 20th Century America's Most Famous Civil Rights Activist chronicles the life and work that made him one of America's most influential men. Along with pictures of important people, places, and events, you will learn about Du Bois like never before.

W. E. B. Du Bois: The Life and Legacy of Early 20th Century America's Most Famous Civil Rights Activist

About Charles River Editors

Introduction

    Du Bois' Early Years and Education

    Du Bois' Work in Atlanta

    Niagara and the NAACP

    Back in Atlanta

    Later Years

    Online Resources

    Further Reading

Free Books by Charles River Editors

Discounted Books by Charles River Editors

Du Bois' Early Years and Education

"Within the Veil was he born, said I; and there within shall he live, — a Negro and a Negro's son. Holding in that little head — ah, bitterly! — the unbowed pride of a hunted race, clinging with that tiny dimpled hand — ah, wearily! — to a hope not hopeless but unhopeful, and seeing with those bright wondering eyes that peer into my soul a land whose freedom is to us a mockery and whose liberty is a lie." – Du Bois

The history of slavery in early America remains widely referenced in the modern age by familiar phrases such as the nation's "original sin," or its "fatal flaw." Whether discussed in the framework of government structure, economics, or social politics, the founders' inability to resolve the matter has thrown the American psyche into an unceasing conflict, threatening not only the Union's tranquility, but in specific eras its very existence. By the outbreak of the Civil War, a bloody legacy of the 18th century's failure, racial conditions had only worsened, and the Declaration of Independence, with its overt assertion of universal human equality, remained a mere wish list of Enlightenment ideals in terms of practical American life, particularly in the Southern states. The Constitution had offered no provision by which an individual could be classified as a lesser or partial citizen, but the ugly truth to the contrary was undeniable. Stephen A. Douglas argued against Lincoln for a balance of free and slave states in an effort to maintain the national status quo as the country gathered wealth and power. Such a policy, he hoped, would remain the norm as new states were established. Lincoln, on the other hand, sensed the inescapability of a continental reckoning with the practice, and called for its immediate elimination. The ensuing war confirmed that the United States was no more prepared to reach a resolution than it had been at its creation.

The Civil War's aftermath, despite the Union's victory, brought its own brand of horror for black people in the South. Following proposals for repatriation to the African continent, a move actually braved by a few, the pre-war slave class was here to stay in numbers too large to ignore. The only alternative for these residents was to seek full citizenship and social equality, a long uphill climb for a segment of the population originally brought from overseas to serve as beasts of burden. The period commonly known as Reconstruction produced a state of civil abuse as violent and dangerous for black residents as war had been for soldiers. Jim Crow laws served as an effective substitute for slavery. The defeated South remained staunch in its efforts to preserve the antebellum social hierarchy, moving the war to its own streets and fields. Instances of lynching became rampant while opportunities for improved living conditions were walled off from virtually every pursuit in which an adult African-American might forge a living wage. With high courts upholding the Jim Crow scheme, "separate but equal" became the South's accepted structure, insisting on the former while violently preventing the latter. Such conditions endured into the early 20th century, expressed at times through traditional hostility, but just as frequently through collectively informed silence.

The men who emerged as spiritual and political leaders for black people born in the Civil War era initiated an ongoing debate on the pursuit of equality. Black men addressing white audiences on political and social matters were to remain an extreme rarity, so for many years the conversations and conflicts were honed within the venues of black culture. Tenets and strategies within the equality movement produced a racial think tank, a hybrid of spiritual, intellectual, militant, and vocation-oriented forces, and two starkly contrasting paths emerged in the quest for racial equality.

In the first years, open rebellion took a back seat to an elevation of vocational expertise in order to recast black Americans in a new and improved light before the eyes of white society. The anticipated rewards saw the former slave class as newly educated, intelligent, reliable, and less threatening. Within such an undisturbed social equation, the black family was to freely participate in the nation's economic fortunes, gaining access to professional advancements once deemed an exclusively white domain. In time, black workers were intended to merge with white society in the marketplace, and find release from Jim Crow restrictions, including unfettered voting rights.

Conversely, the second, a more confrontational approach, demanded instant equality with an already sensitive white population dreading a mass uprising on their doorsteps. The insistence of immediate inclusion in education, politics, and corporate involvement came from charismatic young firebrands, many of them preachers and professors from outside the South. The church, among other institutions of the early 20th century, was a prime vehicle for social mobilization in at least the emotional sense. In tandem with spiritual unity, the development of black intellectualism was intended to challenge white predominance in pursuit of executive levels of employment and to encourage the pride of outright ownership.

It was in this context that W. E. B. Du Bois, one of the men who would so influentially shape the debate, was born in Great Barrington, Massachusetts on February 23, 1868. A self-described mulatto, he was of French Huguenot, Dutch, and African descent. Du Bois knew little of his father, who displayed a penchant for desertion. Alfred Du Bois, born in Haiti, worked as an itinerant laborer and barber, and was born into a family of Bahamian slaves. A soldier in the New York Regiment, he deserted shortly after enlistment. In turn, he abandoned his family less than two years after his son's birth.

Thus, the younger Du Bois was raised and "socialized"[1] by an unusually large extended family. Du Bois' mother, Mary Silvina Burghardt, was descended from freedmen of Dutch slave origin who fought in the American Revolution. In the year of his birth, the Reconstruction Acts were passed by Congress, a comprehensive plan for the reconstruction of the South and the country at large following the widespread destruction of the Civil War. Each Southern district was headed by a military officer with the authority to appoint or remove public officials. Voters were

---

[1] History.com, W. E. B. Du Bois –www.history.com/topics/black-history/w-e-b-du-bois

registered, including freedmen and whites willing to take an "extended loyalty oath."[2] Congress passed the Acts in the previous year, but the override of Andrew Johnson's presidential veto required a second year before being put into practice. Du Bois would in time gain awareness of the semantic roots of such historic changes, but he would not encounter the tangible ramifications for years to come.

In terms of education and the larger community, Du Bois' experience differed greatly from that of Southern children. While Booker T. Washington grew up as a slave eventually freed by Lincoln's "Proclamation," Du Bois enjoyed a far more tolerant and inclusive atmosphere. He was encouraged by white teachers to attend school, and he advanced quickly due to an extraordinary aptitude for study. The high school of Great Barrington was fully integrated, even though less than two dozen African-Americans resided in the town of 4,000.

Moreover, by the age of 15, Du Bois was a regular columnist for two regional newspapers, the *Springfield Republican* and the black-owned *New York Globe*, edited by Thomas Fortune. The slave-born Fortune spent his childhood working in print shops, and went on to manage several influential newspapers dedicated to African-American rights. He maintained an association with Booker T. Washington as well.

By Du Bois' graduation year, 1884, he already felt the influence of historian Albert Bushnell Hart and philosopher William James. In time, both would become his mentors and friends. Among his classmates, he was the only graduate among 12 African-American students. His mother died soon after, and in 1885, Du Bois moved to Nashville to attend Fisk University. Pursuing an undergraduate degree there, the alien environment of the South constituted his first encounters with life under Jim Crow. Established as a "racial caste system,"[3] the accepted way of life in the South was not only directed at specific social institutions, behavioral practices, and a fragile access to civil rights, but saturated every detail of daily life. Social norms prohibited any interracial contact, particularly between the sexes, that could be construed as intimacy, including even the shaking of hands or in titles and terms of address. The persistent Jim Crow codes saturated Southern life well past the mid-20th century, as "Craniologists, eugenicists, phrenologists and social Darwinists"[4] preached the African race's intellectual inferiority as a reinforcement of the system. Voting rights for African-Americans were curbed to the point of obliteration, as the only citizens allowed to vote had pre-war ancestors with the same privilege.

---

[2] U.S. History.com, Reconstruction Acts of 1867-1868 – www.u-s-history.com/pages/h17.html
[3] Jim Crow Museum of Racist Memorabilia, Ferris State University – www.ferris.edu/jimcrow/what.htm
[4] Jim Crow Museum

Hart

Any violation of even the most innocuous aspect of Jim Crow was likely to result in violent retribution. Historically, almost 5,000 lynchings occurred during the Jim Crow era, victimizing nearly 4,000 black men and women. Victims were hanged, shot, castrated, and dismembered, with 90% of the attacks taking place in the heart of the South and its border states. This was the consequence of a return to local rule as the recently victorious union walked away from the victims for whom it claims to have fought. The Reconstruction Acts, with its emphasis on the 14th Amendment, was in effect reversed as the South kept its former culture by changing the semantics and embedding Jim Crow proponents in positions of authority. Technically freed, the South's African-Americans were nevertheless effectively barred from all aspirations inspired by the Union's victory, and lived in peril from any attempt to alter prevailing conditions.

It was through this sobering and horrific stimulus that Du Bois began his lifelong study of racism. At Fisk, he heeded high school principal Frank Hosmer's exhortation to read extensively from an array of fields. Despite the university's location, Fisk was a relative oasis in the Jim Crow world. Established a quarter century before Du Bois' arrival by the American Missionary Association dedicated to serving freed slaves, it was named for General Clinton B. Fisk of the Tennessee Freedman's Bureau, a historically unsung organization upon which Du Bois laid great value. He completed his degree at Fisk in 1888, and was invited to speak at commencement. Out of his growing empathy for German culture, he chose the topic of Otto von Bismarck. Soon after, he entered Harvard University as a junior.

Du Bois' Harvard career began as a joint project, as he pieced together tuition through summer jobs, scholarships, and much support from friends and community. He was the 11th African-American man since Richard T. Greener to attend the institution, and due to his status as a minority, he did not come to feel at home there despite his academic success. He ate his meals at the Commons in Memorial Hall, and later at the non-exclusive Foxcroft Club. Peripheral pleasures eluded him, as he was even rejected by the Glee Club.

Continuing to segregate himself from white students, Du Bois ignored the warning of his colleague William Monroe Trotter that "colored students must not herd together."[5] Persisting, he graduated with a Bachelor of Arts Cum Laude in philosophy. As was the case at Fisk, an invitation to speak at commencement was offered, and Du Bois spoke eloquently on the subject of Jefferson Davis.

Upon being accepted into the graduate school in political science shortly after as the Henry Bromfield Rogers Fellow, his future ambitions began to crystallize. In his written self-descriptions, he characterized his choices as either making him out to be "a genius or a fool,"[6] but his plans were nevertheless clear, as he aimed "to make a name in science...literature, and thus to raise my race."[7] That failing, Du Bois gave himself the alternative of raising a "visible empire"[8] in Africa through preparatory work in either England, France, or Germany.

Du Bois completed his graduate degree in 1891, and applied for foreign study in Germany, a source of much influence. That same year, former President Rutherford B. Hayes commented that he could not find one black individual worthy of the energy and expense of advanced study abroad. An irate Du Bois responded by applying directly to Hayes for grant assistance, and provided him with an already prodigious resume. He not only received assistance in securing a foreign study grant, but Hayes' letter to Du Bois insisted that he had been misquoted.

Once he had successfully entered a foreign study program as a grant recipient of the Slater Fund, Du Bois prepared to study for a doctoral degree from the Friedrich Wilhelm University of Berlin, now Humboldt-Universität. At last experiencing the German culture firsthand, he was far more comfortable in this environment, and he had the chance to study with some of the leading social scientists of the day. Gustav von Schmoller was among the most influential - for several decades the undisputed leader of the Young German Historical School of Economics, Schmoller criticized prevailing approaches to state economies, such as those used in capitalism. Rather, he espoused tying economy to the context of other social sciences such as ethics, history, sociology,

---

[5] JBHE Foundation, Inc., W. E. B. Dubois at Harvard, *The Journal of Blacks in Higher Education*, No. 15 (Spring, 1997), p126
[6] Encyclopedia.com, Du Bois 1868-1963 – www.encyclopedia.com/people/social-sciences-and-law/social-reformers/w-e-b-du-bois
[7] Encyclopedia.com
[8] Encyclopedia.com

psychology, and geography.

Von Schmoller

In tandem with economic studies, Du Bois was drawn to the ideas of Max Weber, often cited as the founder of modern sociology. By the time of Du Bois' arrival in Germany, Weber had also grown disenchanted with capitalism, and he had co-founded the German Democratic Party. He is perhaps best known today as the author of *The Protestant Ethic and Capitalism.* German historian and political writer

Weber

Heinrich von Treitschke attracted Du Bois' attention as well. Von Treitschke was a staunch and unapologetic proponent of authoritarian power, with no cumbersome and divisive parliamentary checks. Du Bois' later admiration for the strongmen of Russia, Stalin in particular, likely found its roots during these studies that exhibited a general disdain for Western democracy.

Du Bois' Work in Atlanta

"Between me and the other world there is ever an unasked question: ... How does it feel to be a problem? ... One ever feels his two-ness,–an American, a Negro; two souls, two thoughts, two unreconciled strivings; two warring ideals in one dark body, whose dogged strength alone keeps it from being torn asunder ... He would not Africanize America, for America has too much to teach the world and Africa. He would not bleach his Negro soul in a flood of white Americanism, for he knows that Negro blood has a message for the world. He simply wishes to make it possible for a man to be both a Negro and an American, without being cursed and spit upon by his fellows, without having the doors of Opportunity closed roughly in his face." – Du Bois, 1897

Du Bois, having found his niche, was disappointed to fall short of the residency requirements, preventing him from finishing an advanced degree in Germany. With no alternative, he returned to the United States, first to Great Barrington and then to Xenia, Ohio, where he taught classics at Wilberforce University. He described this period as a time in which nothing of note occurred in his creative process, and his salary was a mere $800 per year. In that time, he turned down offers from Lincoln University in Missouri and from Booker T. Washington's labor of love, Tuskegee University in Alabama.

If any bright light existed for Du Bois in Ohio, it was the presence of Alexander Crummell, who defied racial barriers to become an Episcopal priest. The first black graduate of the University of Cambridge, Crummell helped to fuel Du Bois' interest in the state of Liberia, and heightened the vision of unified states of the African continent, on the premise that "morals and ideas"[9] were prerequisite to social change. In his final year at Wilberforce, Du Bois met and married student Nina Gomer at her family home in Cedar Rapids, Iowa.

Crummell

---

[9] Thomas C. Holt, About W. E. B. Du Bois, W. E. B. Du Bois Research Institute at the Hutchins Center – www.hutchinscenter.fas.harvard.edu/dubois/about-w-e-b-du-bois

Nina

Despite the disappointment of leaving Germany and the generally lackluster experience of Wilberforce, Du Bois rediscovered his academic track by returning to Harvard as a candidate for the PhD program. In 1896, he became the first black doctoral graduate of the university. In the same year, his dissertation, *The Suppression of the African Slave Trade to the United States of America (1638-1670)* was published. The advanced degree was taken in history, but one modern critic notes that Du Bois was "badly trained"[10] in the social sciences, according to the behavior of his peers. While sociologists of the day were talking about race relations, Du Bois was "conducting empirical inquiries."[11]

---

[10] Elliott Rudwick, W. E. B. Du Bois, American Sociologist and Social Reformer, Encyclopaedia Britannica – www.britannia.com/biography/W-E-B-Du-Bois
[11] Elliott Rudwick

Shortly after graduation, he was offered the opportunity to conduct a "landmark study"[12] on conditions of black Americans living in the city of Philadelphia through the University of Pennsylvania. Entitled *The Philadelphia Negro: A Social Study*, Du Bois undertook a project that directly investigated and categorized black conditions in the metropolitan north. In the Seventh Ward of the city, he conducted 835 hours of door-to-door interviews, visiting more than 2,500 households and concluding that two major barriers to African-American success were housing and employment discrimination. The study would signal the beginning of an "expansive"[13] writing career for Du Bois in multiple genres, and the Philadelphia study would not be his only investigation into disparate cross-sections of the black population.

He completed a second study entitled *The Negroes of Farmville, Virginia*, and *The Atlantic* published *The Strivings of the Negro People*, a revised version of his upcoming work, *The Souls of Black Folk*. These early writings were hailed by some as presenting concepts that were "historic and global,"[14] and Thomas Holt of the Du Bois Research Institute of the Hutchins Center describes his methodology as "empirical and intuitive."[15]

Despite little evidence for such an expectation, Du Bois anticipated a professorship at the University of Pennsylvania for his troubles, but such an offer never materialized. Nonetheless, the Philadelphia study conducted there opened doors he would never have anticipated. Much of the study's impact was centered on one core conclusion Du Bois drew from the project: the theory of the "Talented Tenth." Separate from the hard data produced by his interviews, a personal belief emerged that out of every 10 African-Americans, one would be capable of assuming a position of high leadership, thereby advancing the fortunes of the race. Such a belief required that African-Americans awaken to their own potential through higher education and insistence on their place in the nation. At an earlier time, Du Bois was of the belief that only social science could provide solutions to the race problem in America, but after seeing the brutal effects of Jim Crow, he turned toward the overt resistance of the street while contributing to the body of written work on racial advancement concepts. The theory of the "Talented Tenth" brought Du Bois notability within his field.

Du Bois began the first of two long-term residencies at Atlanta University in 1897, and he was brought to the university to establish a sociology program, but unfortunately, the first two years in Atlanta held much tragedy for the family. Son Burghardt Gomer Du Bois died of diphtheria at the age of 2, and in the spring of 1899, Nina herself died. Devastated, Du Bois felt certain that the outcomes might have been different had better facilities and medical care been available to the black community.

In the same year, a high profile lynching took place in Coweta County, Georgia that further

---

[12] Biography, W. E. B. Du Bois
[13] Biography, W. E. B. Du Bois
[14] Thomas C. Holt
[15] Thomas C. Holt

rocked Du Bois' faith in the monastic, detached studies of racism. Sam Hose of Macon, Georgia, laboring under an alias, requested time off to visit his ailing mother from employer Allen Cranford, who threatened to kill him if he stopped work. Hose, with a gun aimed at his face, responded with the axe he was carrying and killed the white man. Before the rampant rumor mill was finished, Hose had purportedly raped the employer's wife and attacked his infant child. A mob hauled him off a train, tortured him, and killed him publicly. Mattie Cranford later testified that Hose had never entered the house, and that no such assault ever took place. She also insisted that Hose killed her husband in self-defense.

With the sensationalized story came Du Bois' conclusion that blacks could no longer remain "calm, cool and detached."[16] Such a realization estranged Du Bois from colleagues such as Booker T. Washington, with whom he feuded openly. Washington strove to develop a quiet, gradual integration of society through vocational expertise that would elevate respect for blacks in white society. Formerly a slave himself, Washington was attempting to guide a generation out of slavery and into citizenship, but with his network dependent on a vast reservoir of white support, Washington was unable to act the social warrior without losing all for which he had worked, including his precious Tuskegee Institute.

Du Bois and his supporters eventually came to regard Washington's curriculum of vocational training, with the absence of intellectual advancement, as nothing more than the grooming of new black servants for white households, even if it did accomplish bringing them in from the fields. He vilified Washington for turning a blind eye to Jim Crow's reign of terror, and he labeled Washington's approach as "accommodation." Unlike Washington, Du Bois had been born free and found easy access to schooling, not having to battle through the innumerable barriers to citizenship. Insistent on immediate enforcement of the 14th Amendment and tangible signs of societal equality, he opposed Washington as the designer of an "inferior strategy,"[17] and he rose as a spokesman for the more militant activist community.

---

[16] Derrick P. Alridge, W. E. B. Du Bois in Georgia, New Georgia Encyclopedia – www.georgiaencyclopedia.org/articles/history-archaeology/w-e-b-du-bois-Georgia
[17] Biography, W. E. B. Du Bois

Washington

As a Georgia academic with an increasing understanding of southern realities, Du Bois published *The Negro Landholder of Georgia* in 1901, continuing his investigative efforts into conditions of the black community. In this study, conducted under the auspices of the U.S. Department of Labor, he strove to discover why black individuals and families were able to accumulate over one million acres of land in the region.

The finished version of *The Souls of Black Folk* was at last published in 1903, and with that, Du Bois rose even higher in national prominence. Over the following years, he would publish 16 monographs on black research in the city of Atlanta, and throughout that time, he maintained an intensive study of "Negro morality, urbanization, Negroes in Business, college-bred Negroes, the Negro church and Negro crime."[18] An autobiographical sketch with purposeful detours through the work of other individuals and cultures, the writing of these years identified the underlying barrier to peace and equality as the "color line,"[19] which Du Bois asserted was embedded in the white Americans' worldview.

Holding out hope for an emergence of the "Talented Tenth," Du Bois wrote despairingly of the

---

[18] Gerald C. hynes, A Biographical Sketch of W. E. B. Du Bois, W. E. B. Du Bois Learning Center – www.duboislc.org/html/DuBoisBio.htm

[19] Andrew Leiter, W. E. B. Du Bois: The Souls of Black Folk: Essays and Sketches, Document the American South – www.docsouth.unc.edu/duboissouls/summary.html

"double-consciousness"[20] in which all African-Americans were forced to live. One half of the personality, according to Du Bois, lives behind a veil, and self-perception is forever clouded by the feeling that one is "looking at one's self through the eyes of others."[21] In describing the inherent dualism of being black in America, Du Bois poetically wrote, "One ever feels his twoness,"[22] and Du Bois further painted African-American existence as "two souls, two irreconcilable strivings, two warring ideals in one dark body."[23] His dearest wish betrayed its own dichotomy, as his separatist sentiments at the lectern gave way to a desire for racial unity in private thoughts, in which he dreamed of the possibility of living as "a Negro and an American."[24] Even within his dwindling faith in the structure and view of white America, he hoped for the dignified life without the contempt or withheld opportunities.

At the same time, black life in America did not occupy all his thoughts, as his mission extended to all African communities around the globe. From religion and politics to black literature and art, the world community of Africans held "common interests,"[25] and if the United States could not lead, Du Bois believed other parts of the world should form an unshakable Pan-African force. The increasingly disappointed integrationist began to urge readers and art devotees to celebrate the specific beauty of being black, and advocated a separate culture with its own economy of producers and consumers. This, he believed, would work best in an atmosphere powered by racial nationalism, complete with a wide array of cooperatives.

Such a view, if widely adopted, would serve as a natural deterrent to Booker T. Washington's groveling, and the debate grew fiercer as these ideas took hold and moved Du Bois leftward despite the inconsistencies of separatist and integrationist thinking. In a rare but vanishing sense of courtesy, Du Bois recognized his nemesis as a spokesman for the black race, but the remark soon became a token gesture. Du Bois could not avoid the self-certainty that Washington's efforts were "counterproductive in the long term."[26] In his refusal to stand in open defiance with the activists, he blamed Washington for causing the loss of the vote and aid to higher institutions, and at the core of everything, basic "civil status."[27] The "Talented Tenth," he claimed, must not shy away from this commitment of insistence and must put the search for personal wealth to the side, including white donors for black causes. In later recollections, Du Bois removed many of the most scathing assaults on Washington and his work, but enough remains to make his growing contempt clear.

In the final chapters, Du Bois described the interior effects of racism on the African-American

---

[20] Andrew Leiter
[21] Andrew Leiter
[22] Elliott Rudwick
[23] Elliott Rudwick
[24] Elliott Rudwick
[25] Elliott Rudwick
[26] Andrew Leiter
[27] Andrew Leiter

individual. He mourned the loss of his son, wondering aloud whether it is better to die as a child than to grow up on the wrong side of the "color line."

The document concludes with an essay on American spirituals which he characterizes as the most powerful expression of music and words on the continent. He suggests that the African-American culture cannot be approached without addressing its religious fervor in words and sacred music although his own faith trended toward agnosticism through the years. Through this, he re-characterizes faith and the arts as political, social, and cultural engines for change.

Not surprisingly, *The Souls of Black Folk* was not well-accepted outside of black readers. The white population was not prepared to hear the searing and accurate account of Southern violence embodied within the collection of 14 essays. Much criticism and suppression ensued, but the work has endured.

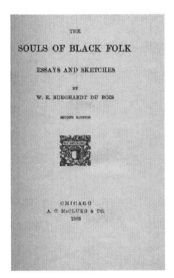

The title page of the second edition of *The Souls of Black Folk*

In keeping with the task already complete in Philadelphia in black districts, Du Bois continued his statistical and interpretive work through mass interviews of the religious views and behaviors of more than 1,000 people. His findings, also published in 1903, were collectively titled *The Negro Church*. A wide array of "beliefs, practices and expectations"[28] pointed to interesting conclusions, but a common thread of unity and social strength was actively present in churchgoers who sought social refuge in personal faith. This being the case, the church was ripe

---

[28] God in America, W. E. B. Du Bois- www.pbs.org/godinamerica/web-duvois.html

for use as an activist front.

One component of such overt action was to swing national black sentiment away from what Du Bois saw as Booker T. Washington's plodding and often counterproductive acceptance of the status quo. The war between Washington and various black intellectuals in the North peaked when the Tuskegee President was invited to speak in Boston in July of 1903. Du Bois' colleague and fellow Harvard graduate, William Monroe Trotter, created chaos at the event through persistently harsh questions, leading to a riot and 30 days in jail for Trotter. The charges, according to Du Bois, were "trumped up,"[29] as Trotter had no intention of breaking up a meeting dedicated to black advancement. Du Bois' ire moved him to assert that Washington "apologizes for injustice…does not rightly value the privilege of voting, belittles the emasculating effects of caste distinctions and opposes the higher training and ambition of our higher minds."[30]

Trotter

The Trotter incident was a factor in the following year when Du Bois resolved to have it out with Washington once and for all at the Carnegie Hall Conference. However, Washington arrived with Hugh Browne in tow, a Tuskegee supporter already selected for assembling a committee of 12 to head research and discussion. Before Du Bois was able to speak, the committee was taken over by Washington devotees, causing the leading activist to resign from the event.

---

[29] Gerald C. Hynes
[30] Poetry Foundation, W. E. B. Du Bois, 1868-1963 – www.poetryfoundation.org/poets/w-e-b-du-bois

That same year, he published *Some Notes on Negro Crime, Particularly in Georgia* through Atlanta University and included the proceedings of the Ninth Conference for the Study of Negro Problems. Among other features was a distinct pattern suggesting that the state prison system was in large part financed through the incarceration of black males, creating profitability from racial abuse.

Niagara and the NAACP

The founders of the Niagara Movement in 1905

"Either the United States will destroy ignorance or ignorance will destroy the United States. And when we call for education we mean real education. We believe in work. We ourselves are workers, but work is not necessarily education. Education is the development of power and ideal. We want our children trained as intelligent human beings should be, and we will fight for all time against any proposal to educate black boys and girls simply as servants and underlings, or simply for the use of other people. They have a right to know, to think, to aspire. These are some of the chief things which we want. How shall we get them? By voting where we may vote, by persistent, unceasing agitation; by hammering at the truth, by sacrifice and work. We do not believe in violence, neither in the despised violence of the raid nor the lauded violence of the soldier, nor the barbarous violence of the mob, but we do believe in John Brown, in that incarnate spirit of justice, that hatred of a lie, that willingness to sacrifice money, reputation, and life itself on the altar of right. And here on the scene of John Brown's martyrdom we reconsecrate ourselves, our honor, our property to the final emancipation of the race which John Brown died to make free." – Du Bois, The Niagara Movement Speech (1905)

Attacking the accommodating nature of Washington's ideology on a regular basis, Du Bois' call for activism and higher education grew louder by 1905, the year in which he co-founded the Niagara Movement. A civil rights group of African-American luminaries, the Niagara group attempted to meet on the American side of the famous falls to form a national black strategy, but no hotel would allow the gathering. However, the 29 men from 14 states who answered the call in Buffalo five months prior met together on the Canadian side. Their mission was to discover a way in which they could become a legislative and social force rather than merely a despised protest force. Priorities included the banishment of segregation and discrimination in unions, courts, and in all forms of public accommodations open to the entire populace. Those less involved with the growing class of black intellectuals often accused the participants of foisting an "arrogant personality and elitist views"[31] on less defiant African-Americans. Historically, the Niagara Movement is perceived as a "major step on the road to black militancy,"[32] producing a dynamic, enduring profile through the century. For the Niagara participants, Washington was the face of the African-American enemy, and much time was dedicated to attacking him as public opinion began to slowly shift.

The movement met annually for a period of six years, but its existence was fragile. The Washington supporters, armed with an array of experienced press entities, ably fought back. Unlike Washington, Du Bois and his colleagues were unable to secure white funding. Inner squabbles and tender feelings were constant threats to the group, and the body was neither able to produce favorable legislation, nor cause substantial shifts in public opinion. However, the congregation of activists did succeed in testing the waters as an "ideological forerunner"[33] of the National Association for the Advancement of Colored People, which Du Bois also co-founded with Oswald Garrison Villard, a journalist from the *New York Post* and founder of the American Anti-Imperialist League. Together, Villard and Du Bois worked in an ongoing partnership as they incessantly hounded Woodrow Wilson to change his policies.

---

[31] Encyclopedia.com, Du Bois, W. E. B.
[32] History.com, Niagara Movement – www.history.com/topics/black-history/niagara-movement
[33] Elliott Rudwick

Villard

Various writing projects occupied Du Bois' attention in the early years of the 20th century. Following the race riot that swept through Atlanta in 1906, he published a poem of some length entitled *A Litany of Atlanta*, a plea to the "Silent God"[34] to explain why such horrific acts were occurring. As Du Bois became increasingly exhausted at the intellectuals' inability to assume leadership of the activist movement, he often turned to more "heartfelt expressions of his transition from social scientist to social activist,"[35] even poetry.

Also in 1906, he wrote for the *Moon*, a short-lived publication that soon failed. However, he continued with the *Horizon*, preaching that black Americans owed nothing to Republicans from

---

[34] Enotes.com, What is the Theme and Tone in this Poem, "Litany of Atlanta" written by W. E. B. Du Bois?
[35] Enotes.com

the Civil War. Du Bois condemned the party of Lincoln and "hammered away"[36] at William Howard Taft for his hatred of black education.

For a brief phase, Du Bois decided that an interracial protest movement was needed, and he was beginning to draw the support of a few white donors disenchanted with Booker T. Washington. As the NAACP began its work as an organization that involved both blacks and whites, Du Bois served as its primary advocate by writing for *The Crisis*, designed to show a generally militant face to the public. However, conflicts with the NAACP leadership that funded *The Crisis* threatened the fabric of the group, and Du Bois eventually resigned.

In 1909, Du Bois attended the National Negro Conference and was seated on the National Negro Committee chaired by Villard. In that session, the use of the word "colored" was recommended in lieu of "black" for all dark-skinned races.

Harsh as his literary treatment of whites was, Du Bois' alignment with colleagues, historical and current, were not uniform. In 1909, he published a remarkable biography of abolitionist John Brown, famous for the failed 1859 raid at Harper's Ferry. In Brown, regardless of color, Du Bois found someone with a passion for "emancipatory liberation politics."[37] Du Bois understood that Brown not only hated slavery as a traditional abolitionist, but "genuinely loved the African American"[38] people. Even Frederick Douglass had heaped praise on Brown by declaring, "Mine was as the taper light, his was the burning sun."[39]

---

[36] CourseHero.com, Du Bois Failed with the Moon but Started Publishing – www.coursehero.com/file/p3eiae/du-bois-failed-with-the-moon-but-started-publishing-the-horizon-with-help-from/
[37] Andrew Stewart, W. E. B. Du Bois and John Brown, A Book for Our Time, *Counterpunch*, Sept. 11, 2015- www.counterpunch.org/2015/09/11/web-du-bois-on-john-brown-a-book-for-our-time/
[38] Andrew Stewart
[39] Andrew Stewart

John Brown

At this time, Du Bois' enemies in print were comprised of a body of white authors, journalists, and politicians who equated Brown with domestic terrorism and asserted he was insane. But to Du Bois, Brown was possessed with a clear vision, was financially and militarily adroit, and made a "calculated stab at the heart of the Southern order."[40]

As editor of the NAACP's primary source of literary propaganda, Du Bois was able to expand circulation of *The Crisis* to over 100,000 readers by 1910. Resigning from Atlanta University, he moved to New York to focus his efforts on the organization, and he published his first novel the following year, entitled *Quest of the Silver Fleece*. The tale involved two African-American young people, Bles and Zora, working the cotton fields, symbolized by silver, the source of both exploitation and financial hopes. When Zora's history of sexual exploitation becomes known, the two separate, but she returns to help black farmers after obtaining an education. Bles addresses the Republican Party and returns to work with her.

After years of academic works and articles for the popular press, Du Bois' first work of fiction

---

[40] Andrew Stewart

highlighted three pillars of his belief system. The first was the need for African-American leadership in lieu of pursuing wealth. The second was the importance of African-American women in the cause for equality, and the third suggested that all literature should be employed as constructive propaganda, an inclination much in keeping with Soviet and Marxist tenets.

Laboring steadily to lay the groundwork for Pan-African Conferences in the world's major cities, Du Bois contributed as a forefather of such gatherings on a regular basis during the next three decades. Preparations were at times filled with conflict, and they were often complicated by the representatives sent by some countries. Among the most problematic personalities at odds with Du Bois was the Jamaican-born black nationalist Marcus Garvey. The base Garvey assembled was for a time considerably larger than Du Bois', and his mission was to collect funds from African-Americans to pay for an all-black shipping line to transport them to the African continent. There, they would form an empire rivaling others in the world.

Garvey

Du Bois was put off not only by Garvey's extreme separatist tendencies, but by the outward "extravagance and flamboyance"[41] with which he went about his business. Among the

---

[41] Thomas C. Holt

symptomatic sticking points between the two was Garvey's comfortable relationship with the Ku Klux Klan, based on the fact the Klan was dedicated to an all-white North America, which Garvey believed was the ideal model for a black counterpart on another continent. At this time, Du Bois longed for black acceptance into American society, but Garvey was firmly entrenched in the movement favoring racial purity, and whereas Du Bois was the superior intellectual, Garvey was a "charismatic leader of masses"[42] who strove to build a unified world empire of African-American descent through "economic enterprise and mass education."[43] Besides their "perfectly opposing strategies,"[44] each harbored an intense personal distaste for the other. At times, the conflict reached juvenile proportions as each mocked the other's appearance and personal habits. Du Bois accused his enemy of grotesque "racial chauvinism,"[45] and he was not saddened to see his ideological foe convicted and imprisoned for mail fraud.

Woodrow Wilson, soon to be president, was still running in 1912 when Du Bois and much of the black population accepted him as the lesser of two evils. His speeches were somewhat comforting, although he would clearly not be a friend to blacks in America. At least, Du Bois believed, Wilson would not reinforce the Jim Crow order, and would not support a Southern oligarchy. The new president took office in 1913, and Du Bois' hopes were almost immediately dashed when Wilson instituted "unprecedented segregation"[46] within the federal structure. He accused black delegations of blackmail when they sought relief from oppression and lack of opportunity. The chasm between Wilson and blacks deepened gravely in 1914 when he ejected William Monroe Trotter from the Oval Office. Local press headlines declared that the visiting Negro had "talked up"[47] to the president by noting that he must realize the humiliation of such treatment.

The disappointment continued as Wilson abandoned his own rhetoric as a candidate, in which he promised an "African American uplift."[48] His segregationist policy extended to the officer ranks of the armed forces. Du Bois believed that valorous combat by black American soldiers would help the cause of integration, but he was again disappointed. By the middle of the decade, he joined the Socialist Party, and he embraced Marxism for the rest of his life. Distancing himself from the capitalist system, he wrote diatribes against Wilson, the betrayal of his campaign rhetoric, and the wholesale dismissal of black citizens from federal posts after his election.

As black activism grew in intensity, Booker T. Washington's policies of patience faded,

---

[42] Ryan CoFrancesco, A Comparison of W. E. B. Du Bois and Marcus Garvey – www.oocities.org/writingryan/dubois.html
[43] Ryan CoFrancesco
[44] Ryan CoFrancesco
[45] Ryan CoFrancesco
[46] Tyler Cowen, W. E. B. Du Bois on Woodrow Wilson, Marginal Revolution, W. E. B. Du Bois, Dec. 1, 2015 – www.marginalrevolution.com/marginalrevolution/12015/12/w-e-b-du-bois-on-woodrow-wilson.html
[47] Tyler Cowen
[48] Nicholas Michael Sambaluk, Du Bois, W. E. B., International Encyclopedia of the First World War, updated October 18, 2014 – www.encyclopedia.1914-1918-online.net/article/du_bois_web

eventually coming to be considered archaic in modern society. Washington was unwell, and he was ill-equipped to continue the feud. The ferocity of their debates subsided, and Du Bois moved on to other targets. Washington died in 1915, and only his prize achievement in Tuskegee survived intact.

In 1915, Du Bois published *The Negro*, a text that put forward many ideas on the true nature of race decades before other authors. Du Bois was the first leading social philosopher to suggest that segregation was more a class behavior than a racial one, and that it was a phase in the process of the capitalist system. Vehemently opposed to the idea of natural white supremacy, he was adamant that segregation was "a social construct having no foundation in biology."[49] Du Bois was so despairing of racism in America that he began to move further toward alternate systems. He embodied everything that was distasteful and unwelcome in mainstream American society, and being "brilliant, radical, and black terrified the ruling elites."[50] He assaulted the underlying premise of capitalism as he saw it, the central pillars being "genocide and slavery."[51] He characterized the essential white American as "hard, isolate, stoic, and a killer,"[52] and he dismissed the national system as incapable of self-correction, asserting, "Capitalism cannot reform itself…no universal selfishness can bring social good to all."[53]

All the while, lynching became a more frequent practice in the early 20th century, escalating into the 1920s. Du Bois wrote extensively on the lynching of Jesse Washington, an event later dubbed the "Waco Horror." In May 1916, the 17-year old Washington confessed to raping and killing a 53-year old white woman named Lucy Fryer, the wife of his employer. Authorities sent him to Dallas for trial, and a 12-man white jury deliberated for four minutes before declaring him guilty. Following the trial, a mob of 20,000 pulled him out of the court and watched as he was burned alive, raised and lowered repeatedly over piles of burning boxes. His body was put in a bag and dragged to his home town, where he was hung on a utility pole. Upon seeing the disturbing photographs as distributed by the NAACP, Du Bois responded vehemently in print.

He followed suit in 1917 at the workers' riot in East St. Louis, where 470 black workers were hired to replace striking white workers. White mobs roamed the streets, stopping trolleys and streetcars and randomly assaulting blacks until the National Guard arrived. Up to 250 black men were killed in the incident.

---

[49] W. E. B. Du Bois, The Negro, University of Pennsylvania – www.upenn.edu/pennpress/book/18508.html
[50] Chris Hedges
[51] Chris Hedges
[52] Chris Hedges
[53] Encyclopedia.com

Du Bois in 1918

A picture of protests in East St. Louis

At long last, the first revival of the Pan-African Conferences convened in the city of Paris in 1919. The Conference was accomplished with a great deal of communication between Du Bois, Blaise Diagne of the French parliament of Senegal, and funding representatives from African-American civil rights and paternal organizations, such as the NAACP, Elks, and Masons. Representatives from 16 nations numbered 60, many of whom came with a promise to protect the African continent while knowing next to nothing about it. The Paris Conference drew up a code of law "for the international protection of the natives of Africa,"[54] and a second conference was convened in London during the same year.

In the following year, Du Bois published *Darkwater: Voices from Within the Veil*. It was his sixth book, a group of essays, short fictions and parables about race, class, and gender issues. He raised the stakes by openly challenging non-inclusive democracy. Although some believed the work demonstrated his best literary and philosophical gifts, many whites felt immediately threatened. The review of *Darkwater* in *Outlook* suggested that the book was "more a creation of passion than of intelligence."[55]

The next publication came four years later with *The Gift of Black Folk: The Negroes in the Making of America*. The book rendered an account of black history in North America and the race's "unsung contributions"[56] to society. The text investigates early exploration, agriculture,

---

[54] BlackPast.org, The Pan-African Congresses, 1900-1945 – www.blackpast.org/perspectives/pan-african-congresses-1900-1945
[55] Scua.library.umass.edu

valor on the battlefield, and incidents of creative genius.

Du Bois published *Dark Princess: A Romance* in 1928. The second novel of Du Bois' career, it is said to have been his favorite, a tale of "sensual love, radical politics, and the quest for social justice."[57] In it, he depicts a 1920s American social landscape primed for protest, as a rejected black medical student and the daughter of a maharajah unite against "white imperialism." The *New York Herald Tribune* suggested in a review that amidst all the romance were "rich deposits of straight sociology."[58]

Back in Atlanta

"The time must come when, great and pressing as change and betterment may be, they do not involve killing and hurting people." – Du Bois

Du Bois received the NAACP's Spingarn Peace Medal in 1932, and in 1934 he rejoined Atlanta University, where he would remain through the following decade as head of the sociology department. That year, he resigned from *The Crisis* and from the larger body of the NAACP after disputes over organizational policy.

With the country suffering through the Great Depression, Du Bois believed that the leadership was shifting black priorities away from civil rights to an emphasis on black economic development. With such a shift came a tacit acceptance of segregation on the part of some, a residue of his old feud with Booker T. Washington.

In 1935, Du Bois published *Black Reconstruction in America: Toward a History of the Part Which Black Folk Played in the Attempt to Reconstruct Democracy in America, 1860-1880*. The work offered an unorthodox slant on post-Civil War events, grounded in Marxist and classical German sociological points of view. Recurring themes included the role African-Americans played in the building of America, and the freedom and equality essential to democracy's existence. Among the most controversial premises was that "the slaves freed themselves,"[59] a notion contrary to American history as normally presented. In Du Bois' view, slaves who fled or openly revolted were not merely practicing isolated acts of desperation, but were practicing "a form of politics."[60] *Black Reconstruction* was largely discounted by scholars of Du Bois' time, but it has since become a major text for a "reappraisal"[61] of the Reconstruction period.

A subsequent publication in 1938, *Black Folk Then and Now: An Essay in the History and*

---

[56] Scua.library.umass.edu

[57] W. E. B. Du Bois, Dark Princess, University Press of Mississippi – www.upress.state.ms.us/265

[58] W. E. B. Du Bois, Dark Princess

[59] Guy Emerson Mount, When Slaves Go On Strike: W. E. B. Du Bois' Black Reconstruction 80 Years Later, *Black Perspectives*, December 28, 2015 – www.aaihs.org/when-slaves-go-on-strike/

[60] Guy Emerson Mount

[61] BlackPast.org

Sociology of the Negro Race, is considered one of Du Bois' most important works of this period. Among his priorities in the document was to correct errors, lies, and false depictions made by others in the general commentary on black history. The work has since been hailed as "an exemplary revisionist exploration of history and sociology."[62]

As World War II started and came to occupy much of the world's attention, Du Bois founded the magazine *Phylon*, Atlanta University's Review of Race and Culture, in 1940. In the same year, he published an autobiographical text entitled *Dusk of Dawn: An Essay Toward an Autobiography of a Race Concept*. *Dusk of Dawn* offered a rare detour from the larger picture of black advancement in America in order to explain his own role in African and American freedom struggles.

Color and Democracy: Colonies and Peace was written in the same year, outlining the case against imperialism and colonialism, and offering an inquiry into past African contributions to world history. In a contemporary review for Foreign Affairs, Robert Gale Woolbert remarked that in Du Bois' general survey of "dependent peoples,"[63] his effort amounted to little more than an "anti-imperialist – especially an anti-British – tract,"[64] suggesting it was more of a rant than actual research.

Later Years

"There is always a certain glamour about the idea of a nation rising up to crush an evil simply because it is wrong. Unfortunately, this can seldom be realized in real life; for the very existence of the evil usually argues a moral weakness in the very place where extraordinary moral strength is called for." – Du Bois, 1897

During a gradual inclination to the left that "deepened"[65] his study of Marxism in the early 1940s, Du Bois was elected to the National Society of Arts and Letters in 1943. Du Bois, in his 70s by this point, was abruptly dismissed by the University of Atlanta, and was deemed "no longer welcome."[66] As a note of courtesy, he was provided with a lifetime pension and the title of Professor Emeritus. Civil rights leader Arthur Spingarn observed that Du Bois had spent his entire time at the university "battering his life out against ignorance, bigotry [and] intolerance, projecting ideas nobody but he understands."[67]

---

[62] Barnes & Noble, Black Folk: Then and Now (The Oxford W. E. B. Du Bois): An Essay in the History and Sociology of the Negro Race – www.barnesandnoble.com/glack-folks-then-and-now-henry-louis-gates/1118633741

[63] Foreign Affairs, Color and Democracy: Colonies and Peace, by W. E. B. Du Bois, Reviewed by Robert Gale Woolbert – www.foreignaffairs.com/reviews/capsule-review/1945-10-01/color-and-democracy-colonies-and-peace

[64] Foreign Affairs

[65] Thomas C. Holt

[66] Ronald E. Franklin, Who was W. E. B. Du Bois? Updated Dec. 1, 2007 Owlcation – www.owlcation.com/humanities/Biography-WEB-Du-Bois

[67] Ronald E. Franklin

At an age when most retire, Du Bois rejoined the NAACP in 1944 as the head of a research effort "collecting and disseminating"[68] data on Africans and the diaspora, and touching on issues in the world community as well. As before, he worked under Walter White, and old disputes resumed as Du Bois advocated "voluntary segregation"[69] in the school systems, claiming that black children learn more easily and more expansively under black teachers.

Despite the differing views on segregation, some progress was made in the areas of labor and legal discrimination. As the newly inducted first black member of the National Institute of Arts and Letters, he published "My Evolving Program for Negro Freedom" in a larger work, *What the Negro Wants*. Largely autobiographical, Du Bois suggested that a visitor from Mars would be astonished to see that among the hundreds of collegiate institutions in America, only the University of Atlanta offered courses relevant to black and white relations. In a series of several alterations of his program for freedom and equality, he insisted that the search for jobs in which both black and white workers participate must be "taken out of competition"[70] between the races.

Du Bois represented the NAACP in 1945 as a consultant to the U.S. delegation at the Founding Conference of the United Nations in San Francisco. That year, he joined Amy Jacques Garvey, widow of Marcus Garvey, and George Padmore to sponsor a Pan-African Conference. The most distinct feature of this gathering was that it delivered an outright demand for African independence, wherever the culture may reside. Du Bois co-chaired the first session with Amy Ashwood Garvey, a Jamaican Pan-African activist and director of her husband's proposed shipping dream, The Black Star Line.

Also in 1945, Du Bois began a project which he believed would become the most sweeping academic effort of his life. He published a "preparatory volume" of a projected African Encyclopedia. Simultaneously, he served as editor-in-chief for two books penned that decade, and he attended and helped lead the 5th Pan-African Conference in Manchester, England.

In *Color and Democracy,* the political world received the first Marxist interpretation of the Reconstruction period authored by an American, and the first synthesis of existing knowledge of black history from that era.

---

[68] History. W. E. B. Du Bois
[69] Richard Wormser
[70] WebDuBois.org, My Evolving Program for Negro Freedom – www.webdubois.org/dbMyEvolvingPrgm.html

Du Bois in 1946

    With the United Nations an established gathering place for the nations of the world, Du Bois regarded the body as a potential sounding board for grievances against his own country. Penning the introduction to the 1947 document, "An Appeal to the World: A Statement of Denial of Human Rights to Minorities in the Case of citizens of Negro Descent in the United States of America and an Appeal to the United Nations for Redress," he was belligerent in his insistence that "this attitude of America is far more dangerous to mankind than the atom bomb."[71] The entire document embodied a 94-page protest against racism as an international isolation of human rights. By introducing it, Du Bois once more entered into direct conflict with the board of the NAACP, which included Eleanor Roosevelt. Growing disillusioned and fearful of U.S. power in the world, he increasingly broke out of his safe domestic agenda to address the world at large.

    Drawn further into leftist causes during the decade, Du Bois chaired the Peace Information

---

[71] BlackPast.org

Center, an anti-war group based in the U.S. dedicated to gathering and distributing peace initiatives from other nations. Upon being dismissed from the NAACP yet again, he was branded a foreign agent, and he was accused of refusing to comply with the Foreign Agents Registration Act. He ignored growing institutional calls for his arrest, and instead joined the Council on African Affairs, actively supporting the African National Congress of South Africa against apartheid. Having been linked to the Soviet Union in the minds of many, his support for South Africa was tainted by an association to communism.

Near the end of the decade, Du Bois campaigned for the Progressive Party in national elections, and for the leftist Southern Negro Youth Congress. By now he was at odds with both Walter White and the NAACP Board, and Du Bois accused the entire organization of being drawn into collusion with the Truman administration's efforts to subvert leftist movements.

In 1949, he accepted an honorary position as Vice Chairman of the Council on African Affairs. He came under a hail of fire from the U.S. Attorney General, and was considered a generally subversive figure by the federal government. His ferocious activism against nuclear weapons in particular embroiled him in controversy with the country and administration that had so recently employed such a weapon for the first time.

In March 1949, Du Bois helped organize the Cultural and Scientific Conference for World Peace. The anti-nuclear society actively opposed both the Korean War and the Truman administration on principle. Much of the following decade was to be spent in anti-nuclear activities, and in particular a pursuit of peace between the United States and the Soviet Union.

At the beginning of the 1950s, Du Bois married Shirley Graham, a fellow activist, author, and well-known playwright. Du Bois' daughter, Yolanda Du Bois, also married poet Countee Cullen, introducing yet another Harvard graduate to the family.

In 1950, Du Bois had run for the U.S. Senate on the American Labor ticket, but in 1951, his dealings with the Soviet Union finally resulted in his arrest as an unregistered foreign agent. With several others under indictment, he was denied a passport, negating a great deal of travel and speaking engagements scheduled for the coming year. In order to reverse the government's denial of a passport, he was required to sign a written statement guaranteeing that he was not a member of the Communist Party, which he refused to do. At the time of his indictment, he was 83 years of age.

Arrested on the basis of violating the McCormick Act prohibiting unregistered foreign agents, Du Bois was eventually acquitted, but despite being found innocent, he was denied travel for the following six years, thereby forced to turn down innumerable invitations for appearances and conferences. This included a speech to be presented for the independence celebrations of Ghana.

The National Congress of South Africa dissolved in 1955, and soon after Du Bois began work on a trilogy of historical novels that would take up almost five years and be entitled *The Black Flame*. The first volume was *The Ordeal of Mansart,* another quasi-autobiographical effort. The lynching of a black politician is described, occurring on the front steps of a particular church in South Carolina. Du Bois could not know that over a half century later, nine people would be massacred in that spot at the Emanuel AME Methodist Church.

Du Bois was further exonerated by the U.S. Supreme Court in 1958 after his earlier arrest. The Court ruled that Congress had abused its authority by demanding a signed political affidavit as a prerequisite to carrying a valid passport. Travel restrictions against Du Bois were lifted that year, and he traveled freely in the Soviet Union, Eastern Europe, and China. Nikita Khrushchev received him in Moscow, where Du Bois was honored with the Lenin Peace Prize. Du Bois would go on to make several trips to the Soviet Union.

Du Bois would also spend more time in Germany, where he felt much the same kinship as he once had with German philosophers, politicians, and culture in general. However, he observed after one such journey that German culture displayed a certain "military spirit not confined to the army."[72] He also expressed a disappointment in the "laxity"[73] of German socialism. Aside from the criticisms, he received an honorary graduate degree from the Humboldt Universität, the institute at which he had been unable to complete his work decades before.

Despite the backlash from these journeys, Du Bois was widely considered a venerated elderly statesman and social icon. In 1958, the federal government awarded Du Bois the title of Knight Commander of the Liberian Order of African Redemption, with the privileges of Minister Plenipotentiary and Envoy Extraordinary.

In 1959, Du Bois was cleared for overseas travel. In a high profile visit to Beijing, he addressed an immense audience, and he described in great detail the nature of his paltry worth at home, and of the abusive treatment suffered by his people within his own country. Controversy erupted following the speech in both hemispheres, and Americans were livid at the unpatriotic display.

The same year, the second volume of Du Bois' trilogy, *Mansart Builds a School*, was completed. Considering the pressure exerted upon him back home, it may not have been surprising that he relocated to Ghana at the invitation of President Nkrumah. Du Bois joined the Communist Party on October 1, 1961, and he began in earnest to assemble the *Encyclopedia Africana*.

In 1963, at the age of 95, Du Bois "spearheaded"[74] a protest march on the U.S. Embassy in the city of Accra. The exhortation to take to the streets was made in support for the "March for Jobs

---

[72] Nicholas Michael Sambaluk
[73] Nicholas Michael Sambaluk
[74] Poetry Foundation, W. E. B. Du Bois, 1868-1963 – www.poetryfoundation.org/poets/w-e-b-du-bois

and Freedom" protest in Washington, D.C.

On August 27, 1963, Du Bois, who had spent the better part of eight decades as an academic, sociologist, historian, poet, novelist, activist, and editor, died in Ghana. The day following his death, Reverend Martin Luther King, Jr. presented his "I Have a Dream" speech, one of the seminal moments of the Civil Rights Movement. Du Bois had been born in the wake of the Civil War, yet he lived through the Plains Wars, World War I and World War II, the Korean War, and the start of the Vietnam War. He died just three months short of the assassination of President John F. Kennedy.

Du Bois was given a state funeral by the state of Ghana, and he was interred in a tomb outside the Osu Castle, formerly used as a holding pen for slaves bound for America. Following his death, Shirley Graham established a national television network in Ghana. Her son, David Graham, Du Bois' stepson, went on to become the editor of the *Black Panther* newsletter in the next decade, and in later years he served on the sociology faculty of the University of Massachusetts at Amherst. Graham's other son, Robert McCants, served in the military. The original homestead of Du Bois' maternal family was reestablished as a National Historic Site covering five acres, close to the local Congregational Church he attended as a child.

The Congregational Church in Great Barrington, Massachusetts

Du Bois' career was not only lengthy, but concentrated. All in all, he published 19 books and edited four major magazines. In addition to his academic volumes and output, he co-authored children's books on the subject of race and wrote scores of articles and speeches. His notable feuds with Booker T. Washington and Marcus Garvey are still legendary within his fields of study and activism. Arguing with Washington's position as he did, Du Bois always recognized him as a sincere spokesman for his point of view, and though he considered Garvey to be a shameless demagogue, he later admitted that the Jamaican activist shared with him a commitment to Pan-Africanism, seeking to place the African-American experience in a "world historical context."[75]

The Black Flame, with its completed third volume entitled *World of Color*, was published in 1968 and again in 1976. American journalist Henry Lee Moon gathered Du Bois' body of essays and articles, publishing them as *The Emerging Thoughts of W. E. B. Du Bois: Essays and Editorials from the Crisis*. The great *Encyclopedia Africana* was completed in 1999 by scholars much like Du Bois. Kwame Anthony Appiah, the British born Ghanaian-American, a philosopher and cultural theorist, joined the project with Henry Louis Gates, Jr., an author, filmmaker, literary scholar, and journalist at Harvard's Hutchins Center.

Du Bois was inducted into the Georgia Writers Hall of Fame in 2000, and three years later, a group of events was held in the United States to celebrate the centennial of *The Souls of Black Folk*. Dolan Hubbard, a noted academic interviewing with the *New York Times*, affirmed Du Bois' continuing relevance and referred to him as "the founding father of multi-culturalism."[76]

Du Bois believed that the only significance of his life was his participation in what he called "the Negro problem,"[77] later referred to as the "race problem."[78] In the evolution of his thoughts and subsequent writing, he attempted to remove racial themes from either resignation or knee-jerk response, and set them as "objects of philosophical consideration."[79] Du Bois was, according to philosopher Ken Taylor, a frequent panelist on Philosophy Talk, a highly critical thinker lamentably "ignored by philosophy until recently."[80] Others, such as Stanford's John Perry, believe that Du Bois fits into the history of philosophy somewhere between "transcendentalists, pragmatists, and existentialism."[81]

Lucius Outlaw of Vanderbilt University pinpoints the transition that rendered remaining within the guidelines of current academic behavior impossible, the day in which Du Bois' exposure to violence reached a tipping point. From that moment on, he believed that a "national discussion"[82] was no longer the way for changing the status quo. In his debates with Booker T. Washington and the process of "slow integration,"[83] he was adamant that racial groups and their perceptions of each other were created by historical and cultural facts, having nothing to do with biology. The question arose among such critics that if such a claim is true, how can one claim all of the world's black cultures as one race? Furthermore, might the same measuring stick extend to all elements of the white race? For Du Bois, a color-blind society was not the appropriate solution; rather he advocated the peaceful and respectful coexistence of many people with their own history, sharing them with everyone. Ibram X. Kendi of the University of Florida notes that Du Bois "was reacting to the realities of his time."[84] Racists of that era made an overt and

---

[75] History, W. E. B. Du Bois
[76] Poetry Foundation, W. E. B. Du Bois
[77] Standard Encyclopedia of Philosophy, W. E. B. Du Bois – www.plato.stanford.edu/entries/dubois/
[78] Standard Encyclopedia of Philosophy
[79] Standard Encyclopedia of Philosophy
[80] Philosophy Talk, W. E. B. Du Bois – www.philosophytalk.org/shows/web-dubois
[81] Philosophy Talk
[82] Philosophy Talk
[83] Philosophy Talk

unapologetic case that African-American men and women were devoid of souls, unlike the white man. When one has no soul, the perception of an individual as a beast, and at best sub-human, naturally follows. For Du Bois then, educating the white race as to the benefits and beauties of the black race was paramount. He desired that the world would come to know the humanity of his people.

Although Du Bois' opinions on Washington's strategy never changed, he softened his personal stance considerably when interviewed at the age of 94. He believed that Washington was a sincere man following his convictions, but he had always been loath to admit as much. Pointing to their vastly different backgrounds, he openly confessed that Washington had by far the worst of it growing up in the South.

However, his expressions of empathy always came mixed with criticism. Du Bois admitted that he "admired much about Washington,"[85] but he could not get past the stumbling block that Washington had promised white society happy laborers with no strikes. In the end, according to Du Bois, Washington "bartered away much that was not his to barter."[86]

In another late life confession, he expressed some dismay at having been "one of the greatest sinners"[87] in terms of racial prejudice against white individuals, as if each represented the entire society. With so much anticipation of the prejudice directed toward him, his reflex caused him to retaliate with little provocation, often in print. Among his most anti-white expressions in *The Crisis* was an entry that read, "The most ordinary Negro is a distinct gentleman, but it takes extraordinary training to make the average white man anything but a dog."[88]

Phil Zuckerman of Pitzer College framed Du Bois as a "seminal sociologist"[89] although few individuals are aware of it. The gap is partly due to many of his works falling out of print or becoming increasingly difficult to locate. Similarly, many of the most telling excerpts were delivered in spontaneous speeches. As a religious sociologist, Du Bois personally moved from "faithful Christian to a skeptical agnostic,"[90] but even at the low point of his inner state of faith, he recognized the church as an instrument for change. Its functions reached into so many areas of black life that, in his words, the organization was "almost political."[91] Of equal importance to Du Bois was that the black church was "one realm in which the enslaved Africans maintained a modicum of agency."[92]

---

[84] Philosophy Talk
[85] Ralph McGill, W. E. B. Du Bois, Interview, November 1965, The Atlantic/ www.theatlantic.com/past/docs/unbound/flashbacks/black/mcgill.htm
[86] Ralph McGill
[87] Ralph McGill
[88] Ralph McGill
[89] Phil Zuckerman, The Sociology of Religion of W. E. B. Du Bois, *Sociology of Religion*, Vol. 63 No. 2 (Summer, 2002) Oxford University Press, pp239-253,
[90] Phil Zuckerman
[91] Phil Zuckerman

In Zuckerman's words, Du Bois was not a "car window"[93] sociologist, and could not tackle such a vast topic without having his hands on and in it. As a more private intellectual, this ruffled his personal sensibilities somewhat. Du Bois was uncomfortable with the overtly emotional forms of praise to be found across the country. In one entry, he noted that at the end of services held at St. Anne's Primitive Baptist, a formalized dance was customary. Fascinated, he witnessed this phenomenon commonly known as "Rocking Daniel."[94] Careful not to dismiss such outward forms of worship, he nevertheless ascribed it to an expression of cultural immaturity, and concluded that black Americans were given citizenship before they were truly prepared for it.

Agnostic or not, Du Bois was forever "sympathetic to social Christianity,"[95] and intended to mine the church's social assets for a national consensus. Even so, he was somewhat leery of the "passivity implicit in Christian doctrine,"[96] replete with a Messiah urging his followers to turn the other cheek. As the political component of the nation split into camps of liberal to conservative and varying degrees along the spectrum, so did the church. According to Anna Julia Cooper, black activist and noted scholar, the overly emotive style that struck Du Bois as so "ludicrous [and] semi-civilized"[97] caused him to conclude that it was the result of insufficient social programs to raise the intellectual level of black worshippers.

Du Bois' "Talented Tenth" idea, intended as an inspiration for the most engaged members of his community, caused immediate controversy. He called for a wave of college-educated African-Americans to take charge of their race's leadership, but not in an exclusionary manner. Just as white founders had, Du Bois' vision was to place black fortunes in the hands of a "talented educated minority."[98] This met with immediate resistance from Washington supporters who cast them as a society of elites. The added charge was that only those of means, not just academic prowess, could fill such positions. The result would be a natural inclination to seek "individual gain at the expense of the masses."[99] Du Bois, who clearly outlined the laying aside of commercial interests for the spirit of advancement for his people, objected to the notion of economic corruption among his hypothetical leaders, adding that the criticisms are "unfair to my meaning."[100] The candidates for leadership must not only be college-educated, Du Bois believed, but must have "chosen the world of ideas"[101] as a life path over personal gain. He did not deny that other options for a career path were available, and that the world would always be in need of Washington's vocational laborers. However, leadership depended upon intellectual might as well

---

[92] Phil Zuckerman
[93] Phil Zuckerman
[94] Phil Zuckerman
[95] Barbara Dianne Savage, W. E. B. Du Bois and "the Negro Church", *The Annals of the American Academy of Political and Social Science*, vol. 568, *The Study of African American Problems: W. E. B. Du Bois' Agenda, Then and Now* (March, 2000) pp235-249
[96] Barbara Dianne Savage
[97] Barbara Dianne Savage
[98] Barbara Dianne Savage
[99] Barbara Dianne Savage
[100] Barbara Dianne Savage
[101] Barbara Dianne Savage

as character. Thus, in the profile of a black leader, the "Talented Tenth" was not in any way an elitist concept, but "a responsibility."[102]

Jessie P. Guzman of the Tuskegee Institute describes Du Bois as "the deepest scholar and most gifted writer in Atlanta."[103] In keeping with the highly refined university system in Germany, Du Bois followed the "German standards of scholarship"[104] before rewriting the text for readability. At the heart of Du Bois' view of the American condition was a belief that the Constitutional Convention's compromise on slavery as a means of preserving a severely flawed Union was "a great political mistake."[105] Bernard C. Steiner of Johns Hopkins University objected to Du Bois' notion that the establishment of the Union should not have proceeded, and that the scholar is "too severe"[106] in his criticism of the Founding Fathers. Steiner instead claimed the advantages of such a Union were so vast, and its "achievability so narrow."[107]

Whether blatantly revisionist or not, Du Bois was equally adamant that the slaves were not freed by whites, and that they indeed won the Civil War without assistance, by use of a general strike. Lamentably, in Du Bois' view, once throwing off the yoke of Southern plantations, African-Americans gave themselves over to the North's leaders. An added point was offered as a tribute to the Freedmen's Bureau, what Du Bois called the greatest "social uplift"[108] ever attempted and fulfilled in the history of America. He believed that the best opportunity for a labor movement backed by strong unions came and went in the South, without the people or Southern leadership realizing it. The apathy and resistance toward such an effective state of organization was, Du Bois believed, fueled by Washington and his vocational fixation.

Regarding the state of suffrage for blacks in the South, Du Bois believed that the pursuit of that right failed because it was "overthrown by force,"[109] even in the North, where the question was seen as the "survival of the fittest."[110] However, such was not the history handed down to future generations. Du Bois reviled historians dealing with Reconstruction, due to their numerous volumes of one-sided, partisan writing. He cited one from a sense of extraordinary outrage that asserts that black codes in the South were "reasonable, temperate and kindly…in the main necessary."[111] In *Black Reconstruction*, he railed against the false, misleading, and incomplete education offered to children on the subject of black history, particularly as it was lived in the United States. In a summary of despair, he ominously observed, "Either America will destroy

---

[102] Lynn Neary, , W. E. B. Du Bois Dies at 150, *PBS.org, morning Edition*, Feb. 22, 2018 – www.npr.org/2018/02/22/587839970/w-e-b-du-bois-at-150

[103] Jessie P. Guzman, W. E. B. Du Bois – the Historian, *The Journal of Negro Educators*, Vol. 30 No. 4 (Autumn, 1961) pp377-385

[104] Jessie P. Guzman

[105] Jessie P. Guzman

[106] Jessie P. Guzman

[107] Jessie P. Guzman

[108] Jessie P. Guzman

[109] Jessie P. Guzman

[110] Jessie P. Guzman

[111] Jessie P. Guzman

ignorance, or ignorance will destroy America."[112]

Sterling D. Spero, a scholar in public administration at New York University, pushed back on the incessantly extreme nature of Du Bois' writing. Spero suggests that Du Bois, after establishing an important thesis, got off track due to an obsession with abuse, abandoning a calmer study of the larger history. Others carry Spero's point further by declining to characterize *Black Reconstruction* as history at all, labeling it as an exercise in bitterness against real injustices and prejudice. Nonetheless, regardless of his standards of research, Du Bois is regarded by some as a fine scholar with a "bad temper."[113]

Abram L. Harris, a prominent scholar during Du Bois' lifetime and grandson of slaves, blamed the single-mindedness of Du Bois' attacks on the theory that he was too new a Marxist for disciplining his mental process. He referred to Du Bois as "a racialist [who] comes very near racial chauvinism."[114] Du Bois admitted in his lifetime that he was prejudiced in favor of black interests, but that he remained accurate in his academic integrity. Whether embracing Washington's vocational path or his own intellectual program, Du Bois was fierce in his belief that "to be a poor man is hard, but to be a poor race in a land of dollars is the very bottom of hardships."[115] He stood behind *Black Reconstruction* as a document that restores the balance of ill-revised history.

The criticisms continue to accumulate, with one historian admitting that the "wizardry of [Du Bois'] words"[116] are blinding, but that such a degree of passion and bitterness disqualifies him from interpreting the facts. He is, while a magnificent lawyer for the defense, an unfit judge. But even these scathing responses become more tranquil in summarizing Du Bois' general body of work, and many historians, philosophers, and cultural sociologists accept the proposal that more is owed to him in terms of literary values and scholarly achievements than to any other African-American individual. Indeed, over 50 years after his death, Du Bois is increasingly lauded not only as one of the most influential black men in American history, but one of the most seminal figures of the 20th century.

Online Resources

Other books about 19th century America by Charles River Editors

Other books about 20th century America by Charles River Editors

Other books about Du Bois on Amazon

---

[112] AZ Quotes, W. E. B. Quotes – www.azquotes.com/author/1590-W_E_B_Du_Bois
[113] Jessie P. Guzman
[114] Jessie P. Guzman
[115] AZQuotes
[116] Jessie P. Guzman

Further Reading

Alridge, Derrick P., W. E. B. Du Bois in Georgia, New Georgia Encyclopedia – www.georgiaencyclopedia.org/articles/history-archaeology/w-e-b-du-bois-Georgia

AZQuotes, W. E. B. Quotes – www.AZquotes.com/uthor/1590-W_E_B_Du_Bois

Battle, Juan, Wright, Earl II, W. E. B. Du Bois' Talented Tenth: A Quantitative Assessment, *Journal of Black Studies*, Vol. 32 No. 6 (July 2002)

Biography, W. E. B. Du Bois – www.biography.com/people/web/du-bois-9279924

BlackPast.org, Du Bois, William Edward Burghardt (1868-1963) – www.blackpast.org/aah/dubois-william-edward-burghardt-1863-1963

Cofrancesco, Ryan, A Comparison of W. E. B. Du Bois and Marcus Garvey – www.oocities.org/writingryan/dubois.html

Du Bois, W. E. B., Quest for the Silver Fleece, Scua Library, University of Massachusetts Amherst – www.scua.library.umas.edu/duboispedia/doku.php?=id=about:quest_of_the_silver_fleece

De Bois, W.E.B, The Negro, University of Pennsylvania –www.upenn.edu/pennpress/book/18508.html

Du Bois, W. E. B., Dark Princess, University Press of Mississippi-www.upress.state.ms.us/books/265

Encyclopedia.com, Du Bois, W. E. B., 1868-1963 – www.encyclopedia.com/people/social-sciences-and-law/social-reformers/w-e-b-dubois

Enotes.com, W. E. B. Biography – www.enotes.com/topics/w-e-b-du-bois

Enotes.com, What is the Theme and Tone of This Poem, "A Litany of Atlanta" written by W. E. B. Du Bois?

Foreign Affairs, Color and Democracy: Colonies and Peace by W. E. B. Du Bois, Reviewed by Robert Gale Woolbert – www.foreignaffairs.com/reviews/capsule-review/1945-10-1/color=and-democracy-colonies-and-peace

Franklin, Ronald E., Who Was W. E. B. Du Bois? Updated Dec. 1, 2017, Owlcation – www.owlcation.com/humanities/Biography-WEB-Du-Bois

God in America, W. E. B. Du Bois – www.pbs.org/godinamerica/Web-dubois.html

Guzman, Jessie P., W. E. B. Du Bois – The Historian – *The Journal of Negro Education*, Vol. 30 No. 4 (Autumn, 1961)

Hedges, Chris, The Second Sight of W. E. B. Du Bois, Truthdig.com, June 30, 2018 – www.truthdig.com/articles/the-second-sight-of-w-e-b-du-bois

History.com, W. E. B. Du Bois – www.history.com/topics/black-history/w-e-b-du-bois

Holt, Thomas C. About W. E. B. Du Bois, W. E. B. Du Bois Research Institute at the Hutchins Center – www.hutchinscenter.fas.harvard.edu/dubious/about-w-e-b-du-bois

Hynes, Gerald C. Hynes, A Biographical Sketch of W. E. B. Du Bois, W. E. B. Du Bois Learning Center – www.duboislc.org/html/DuBoisBio.html;

JBHE Foundation, Inc., W. E. B. at Harvard, *The Journal of Blacks in Higher Education*, No. 15 (Spring, 1997)

Jim Crow Museum of Racist Memorabilia, Ferris State University – www.ferris.edu/jimcrow/what.htm

Leiter, Andrew, W. E. B. Du Bois, The Souls of Black Folk: Essays and Sketches, Documenting the American South – www.docsouth.unc.edu/duboissouls/summary.html

McGill, Ralph, W. E. B. Du Bois, Interview, November, 1965, The Atlantic – www.theatlantic.com/past/docs/unbound/flashlbks/black.mcgill.htm

Mount, Guy Emerson, When Slaves Go On Strike: W. E. B. Du Bois' Black Reconstruction 80 Years Later, December 28. 2015 – www.aaihs.org/when-slaves-go-on-strike/

Neary Lynn, PBS.org, W. E. B. Du Bois Dies at 150. Feb. 22, 2018, Morning Edition – www.npr.org/2018/02/22/587839970/w-e-b-du-bois-at-150

NNDB, W. E. B. Du Bois – www.nndb.com/people/535/000031442/

Poetry Foundation, W. E. B. Du Bois, 1868-1963 – www.petryfoundation.org/poet/w-e-b-du-bois

Philosophy Talk, W. E. B. Du-Bois – www.philosophytalk.org/shows/web-dubois

Rudwick, Eliott, W. E. B. Du Bois, American Sociologist and Social Reformer, Encyclopaedia Britannica – www.britannica.com/biography/W-E-B-Du-Bois

Sambaluk, Nicholas Michael, Du Bois, W. E. B., International Encyclopedia of the First World War, Updated October 18, 2014 – www.encyclopedia,1914-1918-online.net/article/du_bois_web

Savage, Barbara Dianne, W. E. B. Du Bois and "The Negro Church," *The Annals of the American Academy of Political and Social Science*, Vol. 568, *The Study of African-American Problems: W. E. B. Du Bois' Agenda, Then and Now* (March, 2000)

Standard Encyclopedia of Philosophy W. E. B. Du Bois – www.plato.tanford.edu/entries/dubois/

Stewart, Andrew, W. E. B. Du Bois on John Brown: A Book for Our Time, Sept. 11, 2015, *Counterpunch* – www.counterpunch.org/2015/09/11/eb-du-bois-on-john-brown-a-book-for-out-time/

U.S. History.com, The Reconstruction Acts of 1867-1868 – www.u-s-history.com/pages/h417.html

WebDuBois.org, My Evolving Program for Negro Freedom – www.webdubois.org/dbMyEvolvingPrgm.html

Wormser, Richard, W. E. B. Du Bois, 1868-1863 – www.thirteen.org/wnet/jimcrow/stories_people_dubois.html

Zuckerman, Phil, The Sociology of Religion of W. E. B. Du Bois, *Sociology of Religion*, Vol. 63, No. 2 (Summer 2002), Oxford University Press

Free Books by Charles River Editors

We have brand new titles available for free most days of the week. To see which of our titles are currently free, click on this link.

Discounted Books by Charles River Editors

We have titles at a discount price of just 99 cents everyday. To see which of our titles are currently 99 cents, click on this link.

Made in the USA
Columbia, SC
20 June 2025